LOCH NESS MONSTER

CHRISTOPHER BAHN

CREATIVE EDUCATION • CREATIVE PAPERBACKS

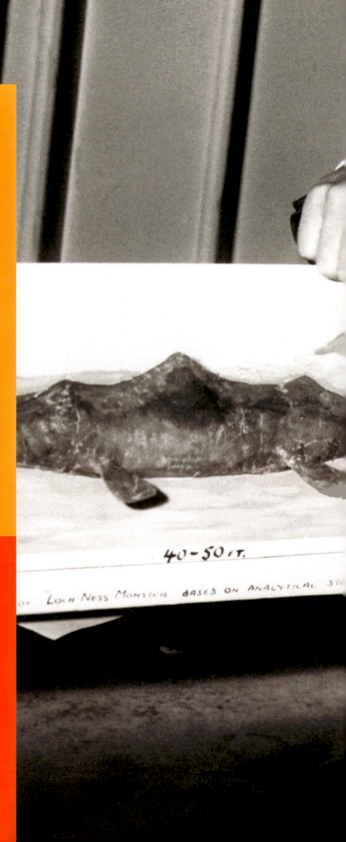

Published by Creative Education and Creative Paperbacks
P.O. Box 227, Mankato, Minnesota 56002
Creative Education and Creative Paperbacks
are imprints of The Creative Company
www.thecreativecompany.us

Design by Graham Morgan
Art direction by Blue Design (www.bluedes.com)

Images by Adobe Illustrator/AI Generated, 17; Alamy Stock Photo/Alex Mustard, 28, KEYSTONE Pictures USA, 36, Mark Boulton, 31; flickr/Biodiversity Heritage Library, 12, 20; Getty Images/Bettmann, 4–5, Fox Photos, 39, Ludovic Debono, 19, MR1805, 32, MyLoupe, 2, Print Collector, 16, Radio Times, 44, Raymond Kleboe, 43, Warpaintcobra, 24; iStock/Matt84, 8; Microsoft Designer/AI Generated, cover, 1, 48; Shutterstock, 6, Alexey Stiop, 33, Chris Harvey, 3, frantisekhojdysz, 42, M Rutherford, 15, Pics by Nick, 22, Pincasso, 30, Ralf Juergen Kraft, 14, scubaluna, 26; SuperStock/DeAgostini, 35; Wikimedia Commons/Cephas, 41, Dennis Jarvis, 34, Dominik Hammelsbruch, 25, NASA, 40, NASA/GSFC/Jeff Schmaltz/MODIS Land Rapid Response Team, 11, Shadowgate, 13

Every effort has been made to contact copyright holders for material reproduced in this book. Any omissions will be rectified in subsequent printings if notice is given to the publisher.

Copyright © 2025 Creative Education, Creative Paperbacks
International copyright reserved in all countries.
No part of this book may be reproduced in any form
without written permission from the publisher.

Library of Congress Cataloging-in-Publication Data
Names: Bahn, Christopher (Children's story writer) author.
Title: Loch ness monster / Christopher Bahn.
Description: Mankato, Minnesota : Creative Education and Creative Paperbacks, [2025] | Series: Enduring mysteries | Includes bibliographical references and index. | Audience: Ages 10–14 | Audience: Grades 7–9 | Summary: "An investigative approach to the mystery surrounding the Loch Ness Monster ("Nessie") for age 12 and up, from historical accounts and popular myths to hard facts and evidence. Includes a glossary, index, sidebars, and further resources"—Provided by publisher.
Identifiers: LCCN 2024015972 (print) | LCCN 2024015973 (ebook) | ISBN 9798889892878 (library binding) | ISBN 9781682776537 (paperback) | ISBN 9798889893981 (ebook)
Subjects: LCSH: Loch Ness monster—Juvenile literature.
Classification: LCC QL89.2.L6 B34 2025 (print) | LCC QL89.2.L6 (ebook) | DDC 001.944—dc23/eng/20240502
LC record available at https://lccn.loc.gov/2024015972
LC ebook record available at https://lccn.loc.gov/2024015973

Printed in China

CONTENTS

Introduction 9

Nessie Country 10

What Is It? 21

I Spy a Monster 29

The Search Goes On 37

Field Notes 46

Selected Bibliography 47

Websites 47

Index 48

INTRODUCTION

OPPOSITE: The infamous 1934 "surgeon's photo" of the Loch Ness Monster was later proven fake.

November 12, 1933, was a fine day for a walk in northern Scotland. The sun was shining. The winds were light. So Hugh Gray grabbed his camera and ambled down to the shore of Loch Ness, the long, narrow lake near his home.

As Gray walked, he saw a commotion in the water below, about 100 yards (91 meters) from the shore. Something dark and glistening rose from the depths—a beast, Gray thought, thrashing around in the water with its head still submerged. He could see only part of the creature, which was more than 40 feet (12 m) long and had a "thick, rounded back and a powerful tail." Gray quickly snapped several photos.

Within days, the *Daily Record*, a newspaper in Glasgow, Scotland, had printed one of Gray's pictures. The photo was soon hailed as the first ever taken of the fabled Loch Ness Monster. In the nine decades since, there have been many more photographs, hundreds of reported sightings, and numerous scientific searches for this elusive animal, which some say could be a relic from the prehistoric past. But the details of the Loch Ness Monster remain as blurry as whatever was captured in Gray's photo.

NESSIE COUNTRY

cotland, in the northernmost part of the United Kingdom (UK), has long been known as a land of storytellers. Honed in hours spent by the fireside to fight off the chilly nights and damp sea air, Scottish folklore is full of tales of history and myth. Legends tell of saints and ghosts, kings and queens, heroes and fairies, and sailors and serpents. Many of the stories involve water, since no point in Scotland is far from the sea or the deep, cold lakes and sea inlets, called *lochs* in the Scottish language. There are stories of selkies, creatures who can change from seals to humans and back. There are kelpies—horses that appear on a beach, offer rides to weary travelers, and then plunge into the deep water, drowning the unfortunate people they're carrying. The Scottish version of a mermaid is called a *ceasg* (KEE-ask). It is a half-woman, half-fish creature that can grant wishes and sometimes lure sailors into doom—or marriage.

OPPOSITE: Aside from the nearly 100-mile (161-kilometer) shared border with England, Scotland is surrounded by water.

The best-known creature of them all may be the Loch Ness Monster. It is believed to live in the cold, murky, and mysterious depths of the huge Scottish lake that is the biggest in the **British Isles**. There are tales and reports of other lake-dwelling beasts all around the world but none as famous as this one. Popularly known as "Nessie," the creature is apparently shy and wants nothing to do with people, but that only adds to its mystique. For the most part, Nessie has eluded photographers, filmmakers, **sonar** trackers, and other researchers. Reports of its size vary, but it's most commonly said to be about 20 feet (6 m) long. It moves fast, rising out of the water in rolling movements, like a seal or a whale. It disappears like a flash—here now and gone an instant later. But it's far too big to be ignored.

OPPOSITE: Many artist renderings of Nessie suggest it originated in the time of the dinosaurs.

URQUHART CASTLE ON LOCH NESS

Loch Ness is in northern Scotland, in a region called the Highlands. It's about as far north as the North American cities of Juneau, Alaska, and Churchill, Manitoba. But winters on Loch Ness are mild because of the Gulf Stream, a warm ocean current flowing across the Atlantic from the Gulf of Mexico to northwestern Europe. Temperatures in the Highlands don't often drop below freezing, and Loch Ness rarely freezes over.

The lake is the largest of a string of watery bodies along the Great Glen **Fault**, which extends through northwestern Ireland and into the North Atlantic. The portion through Scotland measures 60 miles (97 km), from the Atlantic Ocean northeast to the North Sea. A fault is a place where two large pieces of Earth's crust, called tectonic plates, move against each other, wearing away the land and creating rifts and valleys. Movement along the Great Glen Fault, over millions of years, caused the gap that is Loch Ness. The lakebed was dug out by the grinding of glaciers during the Ice Age, some 13,000 years ago. The two plates below still rub against each other. Sometimes the movement causes small earthquakes that disturb the waters of the loch, causing ripples and waves.

Loch Ness, in the northeast end of the Great Glen, is 24 miles (39 km) long but only 1 mile (1.6 km) wide. That might seem small for such a famous body of water. If it weren't such a windy place with such changeable weather, the narrow loch might offer an easy

NESSIE COUNTRY

13

OPPOSITE Near Loch Ness lie **peat** bogs, which are wetlands layered with decomposing, waterlogged plant material.

canoe paddle from one shore to the other. But its surface area makes it the second-largest lake in the UK. Loch Ness is extremely deep—745 feet (227 m) at its deepest point—and holds more water than any other lake in the UK. That's a lot of room for a creature to hide in.

Geologists believe the bottom of Loch Ness is made of loose material deposited by glaciers. They also believe the material fills the bottom of a much deeper V formed by the loch's steep walls. Before the plates collided to form the Great Glen Fault, there was open sea above them. But as the land came together, it cut off Loch Ness from the sea. Some people believe the Loch Ness Monster could be descended from prehistoric sea creatures that were trapped as the plates shifted and the sea disappeared. Today, because the surface of the land is no longer weighed down by glaciers, it has risen. Loch Ness sits 52 feet (16 m) above sea level.

The rising surface caused the seawater to drain out of Loch Ness. Over time, it was replaced by fresh water from rain and the rivers flowing into the loch. That means that if Nessie's ancestors had been in the loch when it contained seawater, they would have had to adapt quickly to their new environment. Freshwater fish now live there, though the loch doesn't contain enough nutrients to support large populations. Those that swim there are cold-water species such as trout and salmon. In the summer, the temperature at the

LOOK AGAIN

Expectant attention is a psychological condition in which a person sees something unusual only because they have recently become aware that it might be there. Sightings of unidentified flying objects (UFOs) are frequently the result of expectant attention. Many Nessie sightings might be as well, since people at the loch search harder for a monster than they might otherwise. A similar condition is pareidolia, or thinking that an abstract sound or image is something recognizable. Seeing faces in clouds, human figures in rocks, or animals in blots of ink are examples of pareidolia. The brain fits familiar details to something unfamiliar. Hearing words in random noises or fitting nonsense phrases to blurry song lyrics are also examples of the condition. When a photographic image taken in 1975 beneath Loch Ness was said to possibly be the face of the Loch Ness Monster, it might have been pareidolia at work. Later explorers in the same area found a sunken log with a pattern on the end that closely resembled the "face" in the photo.

water's surface stays around 60 degrees Fahrenheit (16 degrees Celsius)—uncomfortably chilly for people—and the deeper water registers about 42 °F (5.5 °C).

Because the weather in the Highlands is often chilly and damp, dead plants don't decay as quickly as they do in warmer climates. Instead, they form peat. The rivers that flow into Loch Ness carry so much peat that the water in the loch is brown. A person can see only about 5 feet (1.5 m) into it. Sunlight can penetrate only a few feet into the brown water, so most of the depths are extremely dark. That has made searching underwater in Loch Ness difficult. Not only is the brown water difficult to see through, but the peat particles reflect light from photographic flashes, so pictures taken underwater are often marred by bright streaks of light. The loch is often shrouded by rain or fog, too, which makes it hard to see faraway objects clearly. Some people might say these are perfect conditions for a lake monster who wants to stay hidden.

Indeed, if any creature wanted to hide from people, Loch Ness would be a good place to do it. The lake hides many interesting things. Nearby, researchers have found cemeteries that are 4,000 to 6,000 years old. In the lake itself, people looking for Nessie have found stone rings made by people who lived in the area just after the last ice age, similar to those at Stonehenge. They've also found a World War II (1939–45) bomber that crashed in 1940. In 2016, pilots of an underwater drone even found a long-lost fake Nessie—a 27-foot (8.2-m) model made in 1969 for the film *The Private Life of Sherlock*

NESSIE COUNTRY

17

Holmes. But no evidence of a real monster has been found—not so much as one bone.

Does that mean that the Loch Ness Monster is just a story? Many scientists have scoffed at the notion of a large, unidentifiable creature lolling about in a Scottish loch. But Roy Mackal, a retired University of Chicago biologist and a cofounder of the International Society for **Cryptozoology**, said he believes there is some sort of giant creature in Loch Ness. In the 1970s, he asserted that it was an amphibian but later changed his mind to say it was a whalelike mammal. He even presented drawings of possible Nessies in his 1976 book *The Monsters of Loch Ness*.

Tim Dinsdale gave up his career in aeronautical engineering to become one of the most well-known Loch Ness Monster researchers in the 1960s and '70s. He participated in several research efforts shortly before Mackal and also wrote several books about the monster. In *Project Water Horse,* he claimed there are plenty of reasons to believe in Nessie: "One can argue tediously about the pros and cons of scraps of evidence—of photographs, films, sonar-recording and their meanings—but if an **objective** view is taken and the facts concerning them are studied, and admitted, there is enough evidence already to establish reality." Dinsdale was, perhaps, too optimistic when he made that statement 50 years ago—but the search for Nessie continues.

WHAT IS IT?

Just what is the Loch Ness Monster? Most commonly, witnesses say it's a big, streamlined, swimming beast, with a small head on a long neck—like a plesiosaur or sauropod dinosaur. But reports vary. Sometimes the head looks like a horse's. Sometimes several humps crest out of the water, moving rapidly. Sometimes the animal has horns, or it has a powerful tail and dives quickly. Other times, it has even appeared on land, slithering or waddling. Its color is usually described as dark gray, brown, or black, but sometimes lighter. It's been called both a huge snail and a demonic, sinister frog. Its size has been estimated at 3 to 20 feet (1–6 m) long—even up to 66 feet (20 m) long. The size range would make sense if the loch hosts a whole family of monsters, including adults and their young.

Nessie believers say the sightings are evidence of a large, living aquatic animal. How likely is that idea, though? Naturalists and others have said the "monster" is far more likely to be driftwood or other

> **OPPOSITE:** As water navigation around the world increased, so, too, did reported sightings of giant sea monsters.

21

OPPOSITE: **Something as simple as a fallen tree could be mistaken for a creature rising from the water.**

floating material. Or it could be a trail of water left by a passing boat, since waves tend to bounce off the steep shores of the narrow lake and create unusual patterns and peaks on the water. The minor earthquakes caused by the Great Glen Fault could also account for strange water movements. Gordon Sheals, a **zoologist** at the British Natural History Museum in the 1970s, explained it this way: "The thing we call the Loch Ness Monster is really a mixture of many different things [which] could include rotting vegetable material, logs, tree stumps, tree roots, gases escaping from the bed of the loch, and commonplace objects which could be distorted by **mirage** effects."

Mirages have fooled many on Loch Ness. **Skeptics** say it's no coincidence that mirages occur under the same conditions as Nessie sightings commonly do. In fact, quiet, windless weather is known around northeastern Scotland as "Nessie weather." A mirage is an optical illusion caused by atmospheric conditions. In Loch Ness, the colder and warmer layers in the air and water can act like lenses, distorting the vision of observers. This can cause objects to appear larger or closer than they really are. It can also stretch them. Small swimming creatures might look much larger.

Another factor that can fool the eyes at Loch Ness is a water disturbance called a seiche (SAYSH). It is occasionally caused by heavy southwesterly winds that can blow the length of the loch. The wind pushes huge volumes of water to one end, and when it dies down, the water sloshes back with great force, creating waves as high as 33 feet (10 m). These waves have registered on sonar screens looking somewhat like long, humpbacked monsters. On the water's surface, seiches can push logs and other debris against the wind itself, causing witnesses to believe they have seen a strong, swimming creature.

WHAT IS IT?

RIGHT: This rendering of a plesiosaur showcases the prehistoric animal's sharp teeth and powerful jaws.

Could Nessie have simply swum into the loch from the sea? That's unlikely. In the early 1800s, Loch Ness and other lochs in the Great Glen were connected by the construction of the Caledonian Canal, which allows large boats to pass from the Atlantic to the North Sea. But the canal has 24 steps to raise and lower boats between the varying water levels in the glen. It's hard to imagine that a sea creature the size of Nessie could have made that passage without being noticed.

The Loch Ness Project's official register of monster sightings lists almost 1,200 recorded observations from ancient times to 2024. Roy Mackal and other scientists think most are easily dismissed—but they add that 3 to 10 percent of sightings remain impossible to explain. That's as many as 120 eyewitness encounters with Nessie. What could these folks have seen? Compiling similarities in what witnesses have described, believers in Nessie have concluded that it could be an animal thought to have gone **extinct** millions of years ago. Specifically, Nessie could be either a plesiosaur or a *Basilosaurus*.

Plesiosaurs were part of a family of sea reptiles that lived at the same time as the dinosaurs. They were long-necked and bulbous-bodied, with two pairs of flippers for swimming and a snakelike head. They ranged from about 5 to 50 feet (1.5–15 m) long. This fits the classic image of Nessie. Although plesiosaurs were reptiles, which usually cannot survive in cold environments, research suggests that some kinds of plesiosaur thrived in cold, dark, northern oceans—not unlike the conditions at Loch Ness. On the other hand, their long necks were probably not as flexible and swanlike as Nessie's. What's more, scientists think plesiosaurs died out 66 million years ago in the same event that wiped out the dinosaurs. And they haven't found evidence of living plesiosaurs anywhere else on Earth. If some had been trapped

Illustration of a *Basilosaurus*

in Loch Ness, that would have had to have been after the last glaciers melted away, only about 10,000 years ago.

Mackal originally thought that Nessie might be a plesiosaur, but he later came to believe it was a *Basilosaurus*. The size is about right. *Basilosaurus* was an ancient whale known from specimens that are about 34 to 41 million years old. Despite its name, which means "king lizard," it was a mammal of the same order as dolphins and porpoises. Mammals are warm-blooded. Their bodies maintain a constant temperature, usually warmer than their surroundings. Mammals have to breathe air, so mammals that live in water have to surface often. But other ocean mammals surface more often than Nessie is believed to, and *Basilosaurus* was also apparently incapable of deep diving, something Nessie is thought to practice regularly. In addition, *Basilosaurus* is thought by most scientists to have been extinct for millions of years.

FATHER OF CRYPTOZOOLOGY

Bernard Heuvelmans (1916–2001) was a Belgian-French scholar who earned a doctorate in zoology. But mere zoology wasn't enough to sustain his interest in the natural world. He decided to research animals that were unknown to science or thought to have gone extinct. In 1955, he published the French edition of *On the Track of Unknown Animals*, which was translated into English three years later. His work provided the foundation for an entire field he himself termed "cryptozoology," or the study of hidden animals. Heuvelmans applied traditional scientific methods to his research but also made allowances for myths and legends, which proved popular but made the scientific community skeptical. His first book sold more than one million copies. His second book to be translated into English, *In the Wake of the Sea-Serpents*, covered the mysterious creatures of the seas, including the Loch Ness Monster. In 1982, he cofounded the International Society of Cryptozoology, which promoted the study of mystery animals. The group disbanded in 1998.

Whatever Nessie might be, its survival for so long in Loch Ness would have been a quite a trick. There would certainly need to be a breeding population of the creatures to have survived so long—50 animals at least, and probably 10 times that many to sustain a healthy **genetic diversity**. But Loch Ness is cold and barren for its size. Scientists estimate that the entire loch is home to only about 22 tons (20,000 kilograms) of fish. That's not enough to keep so many big animals fed and happy.

Sometimes other animals have been mistaken for the monster. Harbor seals, which can swim into the loch through channels from the North Sea, are prime suspects, since they are often up to 10 feet (3 m) long. But seals are far more curious about people than Nessie is. They poke their heads above the water far more often, too. The animal most often taken for the Loch Ness Monster is probably the European otter, a long, sleek, thick-necked, short-legged animal that is at home both on land and in water. These otters can grow to 3 feet (0.9 m) long, not including their tails, so they're not huge. But they often travel in family groups, perhaps causing observers to mistake them for the humps of a monster.

A study done in 2018 by New Zealand professor Neil Gemmell took **DNA** samples from the lake. It found zero evidence for the presence of catfish, sturgeon, or sharks—and no reptiles, including plesiosaurs. But Gemmell suggested that Loch Ness might harbor a population of giant eels.

I SPY A MONSTER

Since the sixth century, when an Irish missionary named St. Columba ordered a monster to stop attacking a swimmer, there have been many stories of monster sightings in Loch Ness. In 1527, a man named Duncan Campbell reported that a "terrible beast" had taken revenge on a group of hunters, killing three "with three strokes of his tail" and scattering the others into the trees. Soldiers who built the first road along the south side of the loch in 1715 reported seeing two creatures "big as whales." In 1879, children picnicking on the north side of the loch said they saw a gray animal with a small head on a long neck that "waddled" into the loch. In 1912, another group of children told of seeing a massive gray or pale yellow beast lumbering like a caterpillar into the water. One terrifying tale in 1880 came from Duncan MacDonald, a diver who was inspecting a shipwreck near Ft. Augustus, at the southwestern end of the loch. He was frightened out of the water

OPPOSITE: Searching below the surface of Loch Ness has gotten easier with improved diving gear and new technology.

OPPOSITE: St. Columba is said to have driven away a "water beast" in Scotland's River Ness in the year 565.

by a huge, froglike animal perched on a rock shelf below the surface.

Until the 20th century, the remote loch had few visitors. Then, in the early 1930s, a road was built that allowed residents and tourists to drive around the entire scenic, mountain-ringed loch. That's when the Loch Ness Monster truly became world famous.

In 1933, a series of encounters and—for the first time—photographs were widely reported in the press. Between April and October that year, there were more than 50 monster sightings. The first came from Aldie Mackay, the manager of the Drumnadrochit Hotel on the north side of the loch. She and her husband, John, were driving along the shore when she spotted a whalelike creature in the water. She kept quiet for several days, but soon the story got to the *Inverness Courier*. The newspaper's article, printed on May 2, 1933, used the term "Loch Ness Monster" for the first time.

That July, two Londoners, Mr. and Mrs. George Spicer, were driving along the south shore of Loch Ness when, they said, they saw a long, dark shape on the road about 50 yards (46 m) ahead. George told a local newspaper it was like "a dragon or prehistoric animal" with a long neck and a big body. It disappeared quickly into the loch. These and other stories were rounded up by Rupert Gould, a former Royal Navy commander who was known as an expert on sea monsters. Gould interviewed 51 witnesses and published their stories in the 1934 book *The Loch Ness Monster and Others*. And in April 1934, London surgeon R. Kenneth Wilson captured the classic image of the Loch Ness Monster. It shows a creature like a dinosaur swimming majestically with its head high above the water atop a long, thick neck. Widely

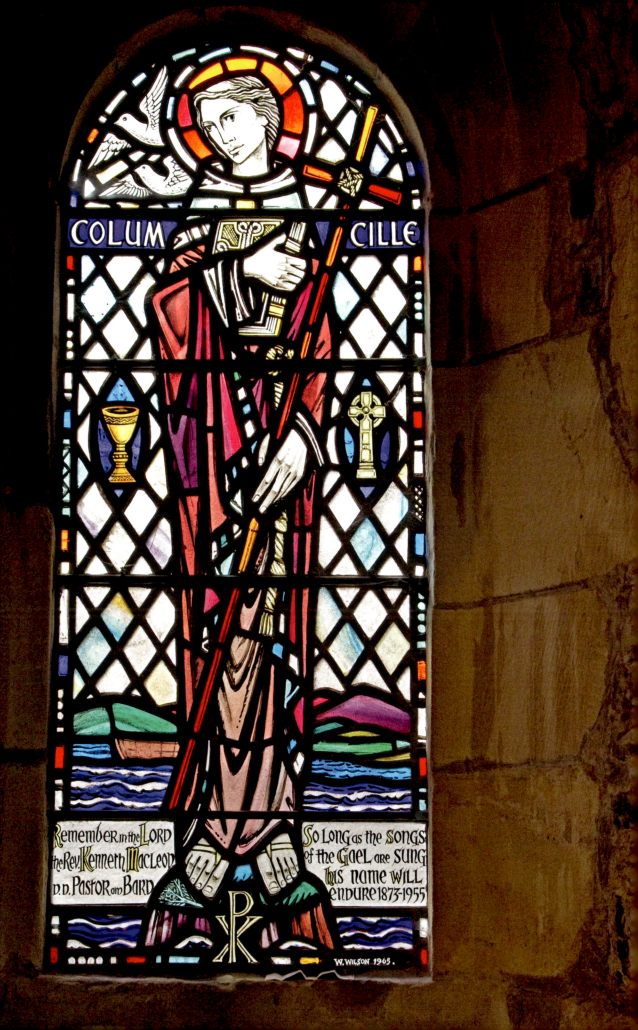

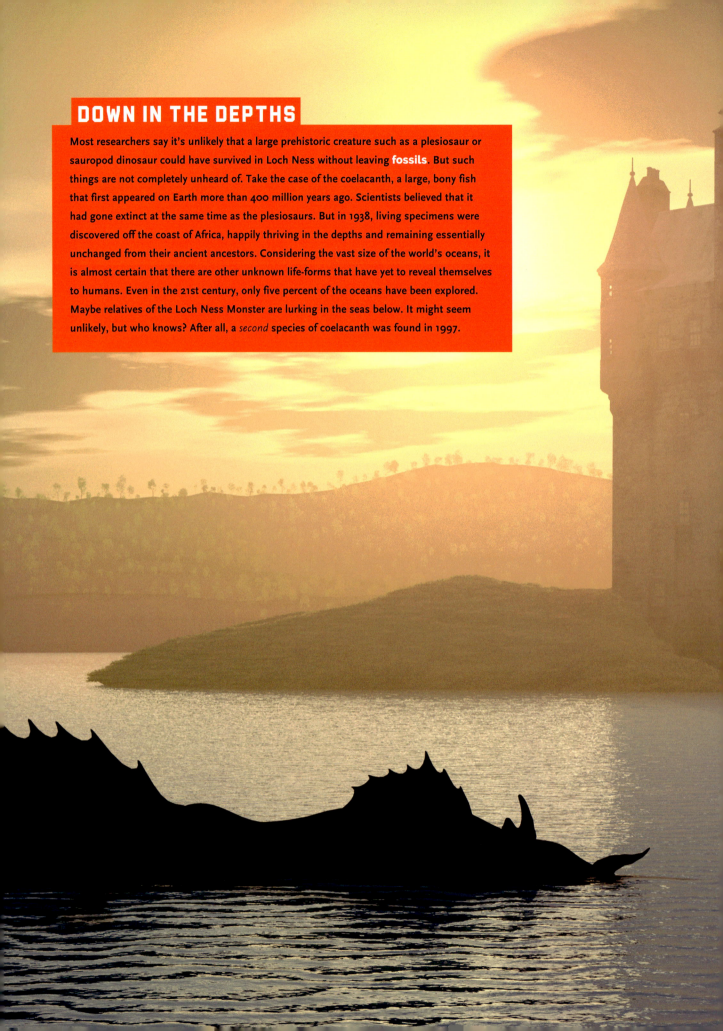

DOWN IN THE DEPTHS

Most researchers say it's unlikely that a large prehistoric creature such as a plesiosaur or sauropod dinosaur could have survived in Loch Ness without leaving **fossils**. But such things are not completely unheard of. Take the case of the coelacanth, a large, bony fish that first appeared on Earth more than 400 million years ago. Scientists believed that it had gone extinct at the same time as the plesiosaurs. But in 1938, living specimens were discovered off the coast of Africa, happily thriving in the depths and remaining essentially unchanged from their ancient ancestors. Considering the vast size of the world's oceans, it is almost certain that there are other unknown life-forms that have yet to reveal themselves to humans. Even in the 21st century, only five percent of the oceans have been explored. Maybe relatives of the Loch Ness Monster are lurking in the seas below. It might seem unlikely, but who knows? After all, a *second* species of coelacanth was found in 1997.

LEFT: Images of "sea monsters" often turn out to be whales.

known as the "surgeon's photo," it created a global sensation when it was published in the *Daily Mail* newspaper. Sixty years later, the picture was revealed as a fake—a photo of an animal neck built atop a model submarine, constructed as a **hoax**.

Why was 1933 such a big year for Nessie? Some say the new road played a role, allowing people greater access to see the lake. Naysayers note that the road also brought potential tourists—and that it was in the interest of local hotel owners to give those tourists a good story that might bring them north to sightsee. Some skeptics also noted that the size of Spicer's version of the monster increased with each telling of the tale, from 6 feet (1.8 m) to 25 feet (7.6 m). Darren Naish, a British **paleontologist** and the author of *Hunting Monsters: Cryptozoology and the Reality Behind the Myths*, has suggested that the story probably drew inspiration from the movie *King Kong*, released in April 1933. The film included a memorable scene featuring an angry dinosaur rising from a lake. Another skeptic, *A Monstrous Commotion* author Gareth Williams, thinks that the older tales are equally suspect: "All were published only after the modern-era monster had hit the headlines in 1933—and none of the alleged sources has ever been found."

But Hugh Gray's photo, taken in November 1933, leaves some hope for believers. The first known image of the beast, it was widely covered in Scottish newspapers. Some skeptics said it showed only a dog swimming with a large stick in its mouth. But even today, there's reason to think there's something more. Nessie expert Roland Watson, in a 2022 article in the *Journal of Scientific Exploration*, analyzed Gray's photo and found it to be plausible—if not definite proof, at least "an intriguing piece of evidence." He added that while it could show an eel or turtle, it certainly "might also depict exactly what the photographer claimed to have seen—an anomalous creature of considerable size."

Indeed, as an idea, Nessie may be unkillable. Although the Loch Ness craze peaked in the 1930s, there have been hundreds of reported sightings since then, especially after Constance Whyte's 1957 book *More Than a Legend* gave another boost to the tale. It catalogued 60 previously unknown sightings and added to the lore. About 10 monster sightings per year are considered worth investigating, according to author and scholar Roy Mackal. But he suspects that only a small fraction get reported because people are afraid of being ridiculed.

In 1960, Tim Dinsdale got the first motion picture images of the monster. He filmed it for 4 minutes as the creature swam away from him at about 10 miles (16 km) per hour. Experts from Britain's Joint Air Reconnaissance Intelligence Centre determined that the film probably did show "an animate object"—in other words, a mystery beast.

In the late 1960s, researchers from universities and other scientific organizations armed themselves with advanced equipment and took their quest underwater. In 1972, American inventor Robert Rines, director of the Academy of Applied Science in New England and a lecturer at the Massachusetts Institute of Technology, led a search. It involved sonar **synchronized** with flash cameras 120 feet (37 m) below the surface of Loch Ness. Two of the photos showed a diamond-shaped object of some kind. At 6.5 feet (2 m) long, it was thought to have been part of an enormous animal. Perhaps a flipper?

Discovery of prehistoric fish called coelacanths in 1938 spurred scientists to search even harder for Nessie.

Three years later, Rines returned with photographers from *National Geographic* and *The New York Times* and achieved dramatic results. One photo showed a bulbous-bodied creature with a 15-foot-long (4.6-m) neck. The other showed what appeared to be a close-up view of an ugly, distorted face. The photos were printed in magazines around the world. British naturalist Peter Scott stated the monster should have a scientific name: *Nessiteras rhombopteryx*, a Latin term meaning "Loch Ness creature with a diamond-shaped fin." But Rines and Scott were met with criticism from other experts who thought that the pictures had been enhanced or faked. Questions arose. One Scottish politician even joked that if someone scrambled the letters in *Nessiteras rhombopteryx*, one result would be "Monster hoax by Sir Peter S."

Naming the Loch Ness monster

THE SEARCH GOES ON

Scottish naturalist Adrian Shine brings a mix of doubt and openmindedness to the search for Nessie. He leads the Loch Ness Project, which helps coordinate such endeavors as underwater exploration, DNA analysis, and studies of the lake's geology. He described Tim Dinsdale's ideas that the loch's walls are full of caves where a monster might hide as "folklore." Shine and two other researchers reexamined Dinsdale's 1960 film and declared it had shown only a distant boat obscured by glare. But Shine gives some respect to the continuing sightings by individuals. "Witnesses are not drunk and come from all walks of life," he says. "Almost all of them are wholly sincere." Most reports come from visitors and not residents, he notes, suggesting that the monster was not made up simply to attract tourists.

In 1987, Shine's "Operation Deepscan" used 20 boats in a line dropping what Shine called a "curtain of sonar" through the loch.

OPPOSITE: Robert Rines was unable to convince the scientific community of Nessie's existence despite 35 years' worth of research.

OPPOSITE: Members of the Loch Ness Monster Investigation Team scan the loch for Nessie in the 1960s.

They identified some kind of swimming creature, larger than a shark but smaller than a whale, but couldn't determine exactly what it was. Years of further exploration turned up nothing. In 2001, Rines traveled the length of Loch Ness eight times. In 2003, the British Broadcasting Corporation (BBC) sponsored a sweep involving 600 sonar beams. Both searches proved fruitless.

Perhaps the search should be widened. The Loch Ness Monster is just the most famous of *dozens* of similar monsters thought to be living in lakes around the world. In Africa's Congo Basin, the mokele-mbembe is said to be a huge water-dwelling plant eater the size of an elephant. Some people have claimed it's a living sauropod dinosaur. Others say it might be folklore based on a now-vanished kind of rhinoceros.

Lake Champlain, a large freshwater body of water tucked among the farms and forests of Vermont and upstate New York, boasts one of the most sensational water-beast tales. It comes from none other than the lake's namesake, French explorer Samuel de Champlain (1567–1635). According to the story, while visiting the lake in 1609, Champlain saw "a serpentlike creature" 20 feet (6 m) long, as thick as a barrel, with a horse-shaped head. That part of the tale seems to be an exaggeration by a magazine writer almost 400 years later. But Champlain really did write of seeing something with jaws 2.5 feet (0.8 m) long, with "a double set of very sharp and dangerous teeth," and armored scales not even a dagger could pierce. The creature, he said, "makes war on all others in the lakes and rivers."

ENDURING MYSTERIES | LOCH NESS MONSTER

People have reported seeing large sea monsters in the Great Lakes of North America, too.

SAMUEL DE CHAMPLAIN

Champlain was talking about a fish, unfortunately. Nevertheless, dozens of monster sightings persisted over the years. In 1870, steamship passengers on the lake reported seeing a beast in the water moving as fast as a train. In 1873, circus promoter P. T. Barnum offered a reward of $50,000 for its capture—dead or alive. Today the monster is known as "Champ," a friendly sea creature. It is the mascot of the Futures Collegiate Baseball League team in Burlington, Vermont.

Canada's version of Nessie is known as Ogopogo. According to legend, Ogopogo lives in Lake Okanagan, a 69-mile-long (111-km), 3-mile-wide (4.8-km), 750-foot-deep (229-m) lake in British Columbia. Ogopogo is said to have special powers and is even credited with the ability to control the weather. Unlike the gods of old, who unleashed rain and lightning but were never seen, Ogopogo has been sighted—as recently as 2019.

Assuming the Loch Ness Monster is real, why hasn't it been found yet? Rines suggested a new theory about Nessie in 2008: The creature could have fallen victim to **global warming** and died. A more hopeful answer might be: It's very hard to find lost objects in deep water. It took 73 years to find the wreck of the *Titanic*, arguably the world's most famous sunken ship, in cold Atlantic waters. And searches for the plane of aviator Amelia Earhart, who disappeared in 1937 while trying to become the first woman to

THE SEARCH GOES ON

41

BELOW: Advanced underwater photography will be key to finding definitive proof of Nessie.

fly around the world, have so far been unsuccessful. Nessie seems to be similarly elusive. It has thus far managed to avoid some of the most aggressive searching and sophisticated imaging technology ever assembled. But new technology continues to be developed that could help researchers look into some of the darkest corners of Loch Ness. Sonar and the Global Positioning System (GPS), which uses satellite signals to target precise locations on the globe, are combined in ways that make underwater searches far more accurate.

Loch Ness continues to attract interest from monster hunters. In August 2023, on the 90th anniversary of Aldie Mackay's Nessie

SPEEDING ON LOCH NESS

John Cobb was the world's master of speed. In 1939, he drove a car 368 miles (592 km) per hour, faster than any person had ever traveled on land. He outdid that record 8 years later, streaking 394 miles (634 km) per hour at the Bonneville Salt Flats near Wendover, Utah. When Cobb wanted to take his need for speed to water, he went to Loch Ness. The world record for speed on water was 178 miles (286 km) per hour when Cobb brought his jet-powered boat, named *Crusader*, to Loch Ness in September 1952. For three weeks, he tested the aluminum and plywood boat over the mile (1.6 km) he was required to travel. On September 29, on calm water, Cobb exceeded 200 miles (322 km) per hour but then hit a mysterious wave. His boat shattered, and Cobb was killed. Many people were quick to blame the Loch Ness Monster. But the true cause was linked to wakes from Cobb's own support boats. The remains of *Crusader* were found in 2002 beneath 656 feet (200 m) of water, and the site was declared a historic monument in 2005.

encounter, people came from all around the world for what news media called the largest organized monster hunt in half a century. It was hosted by the Loch Ness Centre, a museum and attraction based in what used to be Mackay's own hotel in Drumnadrochit, Scotland. The search used the latest high-tech devices, including webcams, sonar, satellite photography, and airborne drones. Searchers didn't find anything conclusive, but it seems that few will lose hope. The official Loch Ness Monster Sightings Register, run by a local man who lives near the lake, lists dozens of new sightings of "something unexplained" in the 21st century.

Paleontologist Darren Naish, whose own interest in cryptozoology comes from his childhood belief in Bigfoot and Nessie, is doubtful. He notes that while such creatures remain fascinating to the public at large, it is increasingly more difficult for scientists to accept the idea of Nessie's existence. He says, "there are no Loch Ness monster photos that have withstood scrutiny." Yet researchers have also recognized that while the odds are against Nessie's discovery, science is required to consider possibilities.

It's a farfetched notion that a massive beast could have survived in a Scottish loch millions of years after its relatives vanished. It also strains belief that a creature so large could be hunted by so many for so long in such a narrow slip of water and not be found. But as long as Nessie remains a mystery, people are likely to keep searching. As Shine wrote in his 2006 book on Loch Ness, "Whether the answer will teach us more about nature or about ourselves remains to be seen."

FIELD NOTES

British Isles—a group of islands separated from the coast of northwestern Europe by the North Sea and the English Channel; they include Great Britain, Ireland, and other, smaller islands

cryptozoology—the study of and search for evidence to prove the existence of legendary or extinct cryptid animals

DNA—deoxyribonucleic acid; a substance found in every living thing that determines the species and individual characteristics of that thing

extinct—no longer existing; usually said of a large group of plants or animals, rather than an individual

fault—a crack in Earth's crust

fossil—the remains or impression of ancient plants or animals preserved in rock

genetic diversity—the biological variation that occurs within a population of animals or other living things

global warming—the phenomenon of Earth's average temperatures increasing over time

hoax—a humorous or harmful deception; a trick

mirage—an illusion caused by light passing through air of different temperatures, such as the appearance of water on a hot surface

objective—unbiased and relying on facts and observations; not influenced by emotions or personality

paleontologist—a scientist who studies ancient animal and plant life

peat—brown, partially decayed plant material that can be dried and used for fuel

skeptic—a person who doubts or questions a claim

sonar—a technique using sound waves to navigate, find, or communicate with other objects under water

synchronized—happening at the same time or rate

zoologist—a person who studies animals and their lives

SELECTED BIBLIOGRAPHY

Clark, Jerome. *Unexplained!: Strange Sightings, Incredible Occurrences, and Puzzling Physical Phenomena.* Detroit, Mich.: Visible Ink Press, 2013.

Dinsdale, Tim. *Project Water Horse: The True Story of the Monster Quest at Loch Ness.* London; Boston: Routledge and K. Paul, 1975.

Freeman, Richard. *Adventures in Cryptozoology.* Coral Gables, Fla.: Mango, 2019.

Mackal, Roy P. *The Monsters of Loch Ness.* Chicago: Swallow Press, 1976.

Meredith, Dennis L. *Search at Loch Ness: The Expedition of the New York Times and the Academy of Applied Science.* New York: Quadrangle/New York Times Book Co., 1977.

Naish, Darren. *Ancient Sea Reptiles: Plesiosaurs, Ichthyosaurs, Mosasaurs, and More.* Washington, D.C.: Smithsonian Books, 2022.

WEBSITES

The Loch Ness Project
http://www.lochnessproject.org
Review a research archive, history of the loch, and more.

The Official Loch Ness Monster Sightings Register
https://www.lochnesssightings.com
Dig into a comprehensive listing of every known Nessie encounter.

INDEX

Caledonian Canal, 24
Canada, 41
"Champ," 41
Cobb, John, 43
coelacanths, 32, 35
cryptozoology, 18, 26, 45
dinosaurs, 13, 21, 24, 30, 32, 33, 38
Dinsdale, Tim, 18, 34, 37
expectant attention, 16
film footage, 34, 37
folklore, 10, 12, 37, 38
Gemmell, Neil, 27
Great Glen Fault, 13, 14, 23, 24
Heuvelmans, Bernard, 26
hoaxes, 33, 35
Lake Champlain, 38
Loch Ness
   color of water, 17
   fish, 14, 27, 32, 35
   formation, 13, 14
   location, 13
   size, 13, 14
   temperatures, 13, 14, 17
   tourists, 30, 33, 37
Mackal, Roy, 18, 24, 25, 34
mirages, 23
mistaken animals
   amphibians, 18
   Basilosaurus, 24, 25
   dogs, 33
   eels, 27, 34
   European otters, 27
   frogs, 21, 30
   harbor seals, 27
   plesiosaurs, 21, 24, 25, 32
   snails, 21
   turtles, 34
   whales, 18, 25, 29
mokele-mbembe, 38
Naish, Darren, 33, 45
nickname, 12
Ogopogo, 41
pareidolia, 16

peat, 14, 17
photographs, 9, 16, 17, 18, 30, 33–34, 35, 37, 42, 45
   first, 9, 33
   "surgeon's photo," 9, 33
physical characteristics
   color, 9, 21, 29
   head, 9, 21, 29, 38
   neck, 21, 24, 29, 30, 35
   size, 9, 12, 21, 29, 38
   tail, 9, 21
Rines, Robert, 34, 35, 37, 38, 41
Scotland, 9, 10, 13, 23, 30, 45
Scott, Peter, 35
sea monsters, 21, 30, 33, 40
seiches, 23
Sheals, Gordon, 23
Shine, Adrian, 37, 45
sightings, 9, 21, 24, 29, 30, 34, 37, 38, 41, 45
   Campbell, Duncan, 29
   Champlain, Samuel de, 38, 41
   Gould, Rupert, 30
   Gray, Hugh, 9, 33
   Loch Ness Project, 24, 37
   MacDonald, Duncan, 29
   MacKay, Aldie, 30, 42, 45
   Wilson, R. Kenneth, 30
St. Columba, 29, 30
Watson, Roland, 33–34
Whyte, Constance, 34
Williams, Gareth, 33